D0554151

Drawing Legendary Monsters

Drawing Griffins

and other winged wonders

Steve Beaumont

Northern Plains Public Library
Ault Colorado

PowerKiDS
press.

New York

Published in 2011 by The Rosen Publishing Group, Inc.
29 East 21st Street, New York, NY 10010

Copyright © 2011 Arcturus Publishing Limited

All rights reserved. No part of this book may be reproduced in any form without permission in writing from the publisher, except by a reviewer.

Artwork and text: Steve Beaumont and Dynamo Limited
Editors: Kate Overy and Joe Harris
U.S. Editor: Kara Murray
Designer: Steve Flight

Library of Congress Cataloging-in-Publication Data

Beaumont, Steve.
 Drawing griffins and other winged wonders / by Steve Beaumont.
     p. cm. — (Drawing legendary monsters)
Includes index.
  ISBN 978-1-4488-3253-8 (library binding) — ISBN 978-1-4488-3269-9 (pbk.) —
ISBN 978-1-4488-3270-5 (6-pack)
1. Art and mythology—Juvenile literature. 2. Animals, Mythical, in art—Juvenile literature.
3. Drawing–Technique—Juvenile literature. I. Title.
 NC825.M9B423 2011
 743'.87—dc22

                                            2010024151

Printed in China
SL001627US

CPSIA Compliance Information: Batch #WA11PK: For Further Information contact Rosen Publishing, New York, New York at 1-800-237-9932

CONTENTS

GETTING STARTED

Before you can start creating fantastic artwork, you need some basic supplies. Take a look at this guide to help you get started.

PAPER

Layout Paper

It's a good idea to buy inexpensive plain paper from a stationery shop for all of your practice work. Most professional illustrators use cheaper paper for basic layouts and practice sketches, before producing their final artworks on more costly paper.

Heavy Drawing Paper

Heavy-duty, high-quality drawing paper is ideal for your final drawings. You don't have to buy the most expensive brand—most art or craft shops will stock their own brand or a student brand. Unless you're thinking of turning professional, these will do just fine.

Watercolor Paper

This paper is made from 100 percent cotton, so it is much higher quality than wood-based paper. Most art shops stock a large range of weights and sizes. Using 140-pound (300 gsm) paper will be fine.

PENCILS

Buy a variety of graphite (lead) pencils ranging from soft (#1) to hard (#4). Hard pencils last longer and leave less lead on the paper. Soft pencils leave more lead and wear down quickly. #2 pencils are a good medium option to start with. Spend time drawing with each pencil and get used to its qualities.

Another product to try is the mechanical pencil, in which you click the lead down the barrel using the button at the top. Try 0.5mm lead thickness to start with. These pencils are good for fine detail work.

CIRCLE TEMPLATE

This is useful for drawing small circles.

FRENCH CURVES

These are available in several shapes and sizes and are useful for drawing curves.

INKING AND COLORING

Once you have finished your pencil drawing, you need to add ink and color. Here are some tools you can use to get different results.

PENS

There are plenty of high-quality pens on the market these days that will do a decent job of inking. It's important to experiment with a range of different ones to decide with which ones you are comfortable working.

You may find you end up using a combination of pens to produce your finished artworks. Remember to use a pen with waterproof ink if you want to color your illustrations with a watercolor or ink wash. It's usually a good idea to use waterproof ink anyway as there's nothing worse than having your nicely inked drawing ruined by an accidental drop of water!

PANTONE MARKERS

These are versatile, double-ended pens that give solid, bright colors. You can use them as you would regular marker pens or with a brush and a little water like a watercolor pen.

BRUSHES

Some artists like to use a fine brush for inking linework. This takes a bit more practice and patience to master, but the results can be very satisfying. If you want to try your hand at brushwork, you should invest in some high-quality sable brushes.

WATERCOLORS AND GOUACHE

Most art stores stock a wide range of these products, from professional to student quality.

MASTER CLASS: DRAWING WINGS

To draw a pair of wings that look credible, it's helpful to study briefly the design of a real bird's wing.

It is not necessary to learn the names of the different types of feathers and their purposes (although the more knowledge you have the better), but it is necessary to have a basic understanding of their structure. The diagram below shows the underside of a wing in detail.

UNDERSIDE OF WING

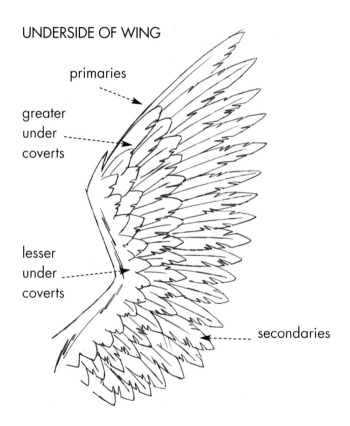

primaries

greater under coverts

lesser under coverts

secondaries

DRAWING THE WING

Picture 1 As a starting point for drawing a wing, start with a stick drawing that loosely resembles an arm.

Picture 2 Now gauge where the three layers of feathers will sit.

Picture 3 Now add the primary and secondary feathers.

Picture 4 Now draw the coverts. Finally add some detail and now you have a wing that's ready to ink.

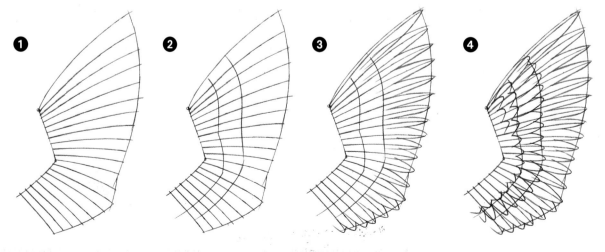

❶ ❷ ❸ ❹

MASTER CLASS: HARPY'S FACE

Here we'll give more detail on constructing the head of the Harpy from pages 14–19.

Picture 1 Construct the head of the Harpy.

Picture 2 Draw the features of the face. Note the large, thin nose that is almost beaklike and the pointy cheekbones.

Picture 3 Add the shape of the hair, which is almost like that of a wobbly teardrop. It is best to start with a simple, uncomplicated shape to establish the flow of the hair.

Picture 4 Now add detail to the hair, teeth, and mouth.

Picture 5 Finally, shade in the hair and face and the Harpy's head is complete.

Northern Plains Public Library
Ault Colorado

PEGASUS

Winged creatures have been the stuff of legend the world over for centuries. Pegasus is the winged horse that sprang from the blood of Medusa and has been the steed of many brave warriors and adventurers. His first and most famous rider was Perseus, the heroic son of the Greek god Zeus.

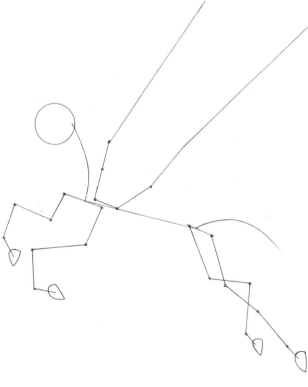

❶

Start with the stick figure. Draw the horse's body and legs in the correct positions. Include long straight lines for the wings.

2
Next add the construction shapes. The body is one huge cylinder while the legs are a series of different-sized cylinders. The neck is very wide. Remember to draw a rectangle for the long nose.

3
Add the head and draw the horse's face. Make sure the mane and tail hair flick outward. Give form to the shapes by applying the skin.

4

Now remove the construction lines and add the wings.

You'll find detailed instructions on how to draw wings on page 6.

5

Give the wings texture with some shading and add detail to the face and body. Notice how we have used cross-hatching for shading in various places.

TOP TIP
By inking the contours of the neck with solid thick lines, you can really make Pegasus's muscles stand out and emphasize his strength.

6
Ink over the final pencil drawing. Use solid black where the mane and tail join the body to add depth.

7 Color this drawing using the palest gray base across the whole image.

When coloring the wings, mane, and tail, use darker blue and lilac. Add gray to give definition.

Apply a slightly darker gray to the belly, legs, and underside of the neck to create form. Build up the layers with light blue and mauve.

The hooves are gray with hints of mauve.

HARPY

The most terrifying of all flying creatures is the Harpy. Half woman and half bird, she is like something from a nightmare—screeching, filthy, and constantly on the lookout for weak and vulnerable prey to slice apart with her long talons.

 Draw the stick figure. Plot lines for the huge wings and include a curved tail. The Harpy is crouching and about to grab her prey.

2

Next add the construction shapes. Build the body using long, thin cylinders.

3

Now draw the face and wild hair. Give the Harpy skin, and shape the sharp claws on her feet. Notice how her legs are foreshortened to make them appear longer.

Visit page 7 for more detail on drawing the Harpy's ugly face.

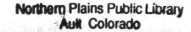
Northern Plains Public Library
Ault Colorado

4

Add the wings and feathers, then erase the construction shapes. Remember to include feathers on the Harpy's upper body.

TOP TIP

When creating your Harpy, imagine her as an evil, wizened old witch to help you bring out this mood in the final artwork.

5

Apply shading to the feathers to create depth and form. Add wrinkles to the legs and feet to give the skin texture. When shading in the hair, leave an area of white to act as a highlight.

6

Ink over the pencil drawing, remembering to keep the highlights on the hair and claws. Notice how the solid block of shading behind the Harpy's legs makes her feet leap out of the picture.

7

Color the evil, witchlike Harpy to make her even uglier. Start with a pale, yellowish green base.

Build up the feathered body and wings with emerald green, darker green, and bluish green.

For the legs, feet, and face, apply a pinkish flesh tone. Follow this with layers of pale green, yellow, and gray to create a sickly appearance.

GRIFFIN

The most noble of winged creatures is the griffin. This powerful and courageous monster is part eagle and part lion. According to legend, the griffin's bones were so strong that humans once used its ribs to make bows.

❶
Start with the stick figure. Try to draw the line for the spine in one fluid movement. Include two triangles for the griffin's beak.

2 Next apply the construction shapes using different-sized cylinders. Note that although the griffin is a winged creature, it has the body of a lion.

3 Now draw the feathered eagle-like head and large beak. Add the skin and flesh out the paws, claws, and tail.

TOP TIP
Ensure that the griffin's beak is hooked at the end, otherwise it might end up looking like the beak of a chicken!

Go to page 6 for more instructions on how to draw wings.

❹
Erase the construction shapes and add the wings and feathers. Notice how the feathers get longer in each layer.

5 Now add the detail to finalize your pencil drawing. Include shading on the wings to create definition. Use cross-hatching for this.

❻
Apply ink over the pencil drawing.
Take care to keep the delicate
quality of the cross-hatching.

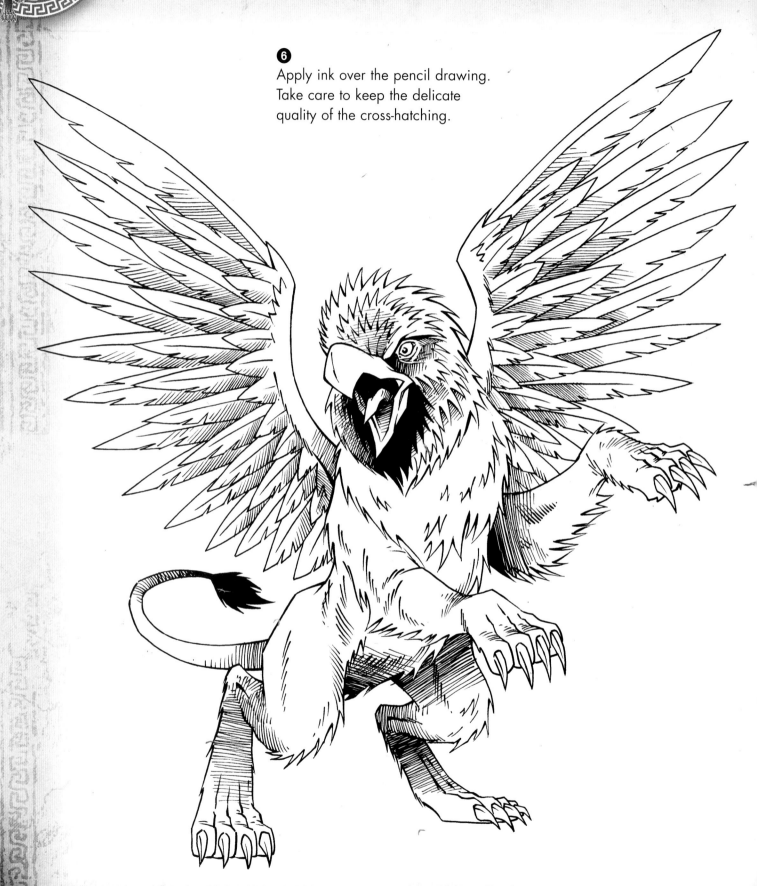

7 Your griffin will look magnificent when you go over it in color.

Use a light gray base for the head and wings, followed by layers of darker gray with splashes of ice blue. Also add a hint of beige.

Give the beak a yellow base and add orange for the shading.

The lion's body has a sandy beige base. On top of that use a darker sandy tone and light brown.

CREATING A SCENE: GUARDIAN GRIFFIN

The griffin makes the perfect guard, since it is as sharp eyed as an eagle, as fearless as a lion, and many times more dangerous than either! In this scene, the griffin watches over a damaged fortress, protecting its occupants from dark forces.

1 Drawing lines of perspective and a vanishing point will help you keep everything to scale and give your image a sense of depth. In this scene, the perspective lines meet in a vanishing point on the right-hand side of the image.

2 Sketch the mountain range in the background. Creating layers of mountains—some nearer, some farther away—will work much better than a single cliff face. Now you can also roughly mark out where you want to place your castle ruins.

3 Begin fleshing out your fort and the mountains. Adding small details into any blank areas of the mountains will help break them up and look more natural. But don't go overboard, too much background detail may detract from your main character.

4 When shading, it's important to bear in mind the location of your light source, along with how the shadows will fall. Pay attention to how certain mountains will affect the light that is shed on your ruins or other mountains in the range.

Northern Plains Public Library
— Ault Colorado

5 When inking, you need to strike a careful balance between the detail in the background and the foreground. Too much heavy ink on the mountains will distract from the griffin itself. Gradually build up the shading on the rocks, remembering that it's easier to add than to take away.

29

6 You have two main options for coloring this scene. You can use yellow and brown tones to create a bleak, barren mountaintop in a desertlike setting. You can also go with the option we've chosen here, of using a greener color palette to suggest a more temperate climate.

GLOSSARY

cross-hatching (KRAWS-hach-ing) A shading technique in which crisscrossing diagonal lines are overlapped to make an area of shadow.

cylinder (SIH-lin-der) A shape with circular ends and straight sides.

design (dih-ZYN) The plan or the form of something.

detail (DEE-tayl) A decoration or the small part of a whole.

foreshortening (faw-SHAWR-ten-ing) In art, making something shorter to show that it is angled toward the viewer.

perspective (per-SPEK-tiv) Changing the size and shape of objects in an artwork to create a sense of nearness or distance.

temperate (TEM-peh-rut) With a mild climate.

uncomplicated (un-KOM-pluh-kayt-ed) Not hard to understand.

vanishing point (VAN-ish-ing POYNT) The point at which the lines showing perspective in a drawing meet each other.

wizened (WIH-zend) Wrinkled up with age.

INDEX

WEB SITES

Due to the changing nature of Internet links, PowerKids Press has developed an online list of Web sites related to the subject of this book. This site is updated regularly. Please use this link to access the list:
www.powerkidslinks.com/dlm/griffins/